The Altar Will Alter You

Lorraine M. Castle

The Altar Will Alter You

Written by Lorraine M. Castle

Edition 2015

Copyright 2015 Lorraine M. Castle

ISBN 13: 978-0692602911

Lorraine M. Castle
P. O. Box 3807
Cherry Hill, NJ 08034
lorraine@castlevirtualsolutions.com

Unless otherwise noted, all scripture references are from the King James Version of the Bible.

Editing & Formatting: Lorraine Castle – Castle Virtual Solutions LLC
http://www.castlevirtualsolutions.com/

Dedication

This is dedicated to my mother, the late Dora Lorraine Camp, who taught my heart to smile. She guided me with wisdom and insight and taught me to pursue my goals and never lose sight of the Prize.

Acknowledgements

Life is an intricate puzzle with millions of intricate pieces called events that are placed one by one within the very depth of our soul resulting in who we are today. Although each piece of my puzzle is important, it would be impossible to name each one individually. Risking omission, I would like to name and thank a few of the people who have touched my life and formed a piece of the puzzle that is known as Lorraine McCray Castle.

Foremost and most importantly, I must thank God, the creator of all. Because He Is, I am. I thank my stepfather, the late Robert Eugene Camp, Sr. and my mother, the late Dora Lorraine Camp who taught me patience and obedience and introduced me to Christ by taking me to my first church service. I must thank my brother, Robert, Jr. who taught me unconditional love. I thank my great-grandmother, the late Susie Cary McCray and my grandmother, the late Lillian Lorraine McCray both of whom shared their wisdom with an ever-inquisitive child. I would like to thank my adopted God Mother, Naomi Wyatt Strange who taught me that dreams do not carry an age barrier. As long as we live, the dream lives. Thank you to my bestie, Shonda D. Brown, who stood by my side in good and bad times – the ultimate running buddie – a true friend who has seen the best and worst of me.

I thank my pastor, Bishop David G. Evans, who allows himself to be used mightily by the Lord

Lorraine M. Castle

providing an example to those who follow Christ. I thank the anointed music ministry at my church,

Bethany Baptist in Lindenwold, New Jersey, led by the dynamic Music Minister Dr. Lonnie V. Hunter, whose ministry quickened the gift that was lying dormant within me.

Finally, I thank all of my Christian friends who have laughed with me, cried with me, and supported me as through Jesus I began to discover the importance of each piece of my puzzle that was orchestrated by the teachings of our Lord and Savior, Jesus Christ. Because God is the beginning and the end, once again I thank God for giving me the strength, courage, and endurance to bring out the Jesus in me while telling the world how *The Altar Will Alter You.*

Psalm 139:14 *"I will praise Thee; for I am fearfully and wonderfully made: marvelous are Thy works; and that my soul knoweth right well."*

Foreword

Lorraine Castle is the former president of the P.E.N. Warriors and L-Y-N-X, writing teams at Bethany Baptist Church in Lindenwold, New Jersey. When I was a member of the P.E.N Warriors, I was a blessed immensely by her leadership. She encouraged me to write daily, and she led our ministry with humility and integrity. In fact, if it were not for an assignment she had given our team, my devotional, *Pictures in Glass Frames*, would not be published today.

Becoming a Christian author was not in my plans, so I was nervous about embarking on my new Christian writing journey. Book signings and speaking engagements were new to me. But, do you know what helps a writer who is uncomfortable standing in front of an audience? Other than prayer, it is a familiar face in a room full of faces that are not always pleasant. Lorraine was that familiar face. She was the supportive friend who attended a number of my events, so when Lorraine asked me to write the foreword for her book, I was grateful that she asked, and I could not wait to read *The Altar Will Alter You*.

While reading *The Altar Will Alter You*, I was moved by her poems and reflections and reminded how God cares about the major and seemingly minor details of our lives. Everything we do is important to God, and he has a word for all our situations. In *The Altar Will Alter You*, Lorraine reminds us that we do not have to go to someone else to find out what God is trying to say to us. In the reflection following the poem, *"Commissioned,"* she writes, "The Lord does not make a habit of giving a word to us for someone else. God will give us a word that is meant to minister to us first and to others later." Lorraine assures readers that God is a consistent friend who always directs us through our successes and our failures, our victories and our defeats, and our joys and our sorrows. With rhyme and verse, Lorraine poetically conveys this message throughout her book while sharing private moments of her life.

Lorraine writes about her mother's struggle with two diseases, Alzheimer's and cervical cancer. She explains how it was a blessing that she was unemployed during the time her mother was ill. "I was able to be to Mom what she was to me for so many years – her caregiver," Lorraine writes. She continues, "God has a way of giving us what we need when we need it." Lorraine also eloquently describes death as "a transition," reminding readers that there is life after death for the believer. Lorraine also writes about how her faith has wavered at times, but she also explains how God was there for her even when she had doubts— doubts that cannot compete with the word that Lorraine has in her heart that comes out in poetry and song.

Having sung on the choir for years, Lorraine has been immersed in God's presence. She is a witness that the altar will alter you. For over a decade, I have watched Lorraine sing on the choir with a passion and energy that is contagious. She sings and writes what she believes. *The Altar Will Alter You*

The Altar Will Alter You

is a relatable book that will encourage you, your friends, and your family.

Shawn R. Jones
Author of the devotional book,
Pictures in Glass Frames

Praise Reports For
The Altar Will Alter You

"Reading this book brings the alter experience wherever you are. A peace comes over you like a blanket, and your world is transformed. Thank you Lorraine for letting God use you! "

~~**Torri Penn**, author

"I tell you," Jesus replied, "If they (the disciples) keep quiet, the stones will cry out." -
Luke 19:40

"The Altar Will Alter You is a ministry of Triumph! Lorraine has clearly decided no Rock will speak on her behalf. Pen to pad her Pilgrimage is poetically documented for All the world to see. May you be Blessed as I have been blessed by her Praise."

~~**Sylvia Sampson**, Poet, Spoken Word Artist and Author of *"Freeze Frame," a Spoken Word CD*

"Lorraine begins her poetic writing with what the altar (not the book) can do for you. Lorraine's poems reflect the love our Savior has for us, and what He has done for us, showing His love."

~~**Rosemary Worthy-Washington**, Author of *"Exposed: I Will Not Be Ashamed,"* President of Healed With Scars

Lorraine M. Castle

"God's Love, Grace and Mercy prevail in this grand book of poetry and testimonial devotions. From the thought provoking, *'There was a Time,'* to *'Can You See What I See: Commissioned,'* my thought processes have been Altered. I do indeed see and hear the souls crying out. *'Commissioned'* has re-awakened urgency in my spirit to reach out and touch others, by any means possible. I have no more time to waste! Without a doubt, Lorraine's writings will touch the hearts of others and promote positive changes to their lives and circumstances."

~~**Pauline Lawrence**, Poet and Author

"Lorraine Castle's reflections capture many of the very thoughts that we as Believers feel but find hard to express as we walk in our faith with the Lord. It doesn't matter if you've been saved or not, these reflections offer a glimpse of her personal experiences of her relationship with the Savior that allows any reader to know that the Lord is a loving, forgiving God and that a relationship with Him offers a place of eternal safety and security. Her gentle encouragement for readers to seek and follow Him is fulfilling her mantra 'each one-reach one' as her words (and the Holy Spirit) serve as little nudges to make you want to restore, rebuild and renew your relationship with the Father."

~~**Belinda Barksdale**, Author of *"Seasons Change"*

The Altar Will Alter You

"*The Altar Will Alter Y*ou provides reflective thoughts on real issues facing real people. Lorraine offers insight on life's situations through the eyes of her faith."

~~**Cynthia Jackson**, Program Manager of *Way of Escape Ministries*

"*The Altar Will Alter You* will give you a look into the various phases of the author's life, through her poetic devotion. It dissolves the myth that, once saved, your life is perfect and your troubles are over. Instead *The Altar Will Alter You* will have you walking away with the desire to alter how you perceive your situation and circumstance, and the decisions you choose to make. It will give you the common sense to realize that life happens, and the faith to know and believe the impossible."

~~**Karen U. Prather**, Poet, Author, Choir Director

Lorraine M. Castle

"*The Altar Will Alter You* is an amazing collection of poems and life reflections that will put a smile on your face, encourage your heart and prompt you to reflect on your life and relationship with God and others. The author openly shares her heart and life reflections in a way that allows you to see yourself at times. I look forward to purchasing this great book and encourage others to get their copy! A continuation of great writings by Lorraine!"

~~**Shirley Owens**, Author

Introduction

"The Altar Will Alter You" is a collection of poetic devotions describing this Christian's walk with the Lord. With life there are good and bad days, good and bad times. What is consistent throughout is Lorraine's faith that through her Lord and Savior, Jesus Christ, she is equipped to handle whatever situations come her way. Lorraine's desire is to share some of her struggles with others who may have the same or similar struggles. Struggles are often found in the midst of victories. Experience taught Lorraine that keeping your eye on the Prize reduces or diverts the impact of struggles. Lorraine's writing demonstrates that her faith in the Lord is the difference between failure and victory.

Table of Contents

Dedication...iii

Acknowledgements iv

Foreword vi

Praise Reports For *The Altar Will Alter You* x

Introduction xiv

The Altar Will Alter You 6

    The Altar Will Alter You...................................2

        The Altar Will Alter You – Reflections 3

My Deliverer...6

    I Will Give You Praise 7

        I Will Give You Praise – Reflections 8

    Long Ago on Calvary...9

        Long Ago on Calvary – Reflections 10

    Commissioned...12

        Commissioned – Reflections 14

    No Matter...16

        No Matter – Reflections 17

    Temporal Things, Eternal Treasures............19

        Temporal Things – Eternal Treasures –
        Reflections 21

    Who Will You Choose?.....................................23

        Who Will You Choose? – Reflections 24

    Even So...25

        Even So – Reflections 27

God's Time..29

   God's Time. – Reflections 30

Sister, Sister 31

   Sister, Sister – Reflections..........................34

The Gift 35

   The Gift – Reflections................................36

My Protector 38

Your Child is in God's Hands.....................39

   Your Child is in God's Hands – Reflections
  41

We Can Pray..43

   We Can Pray – Reflections 44

God Is!...45

   God Is! – Reflections 48

Jesus Is The Answer.....................................50

   Jesus Is The Answer – Reflections 52

He Is! 54

   He Is! – Reflections....................................55

My Provider 56

Christian Friends 57

   Christian Friends – Reflections.................58

I . C . Z . (Insulated Comfort Zone)...............59

   I. C. Z. (Insulated Comfort Zone) –
   Reflections 60

Precious 61

   Precious – Reflections 63

Christian Hospitality....................................65

Christian Hospitality – Reflections 66

The Lord is Her All in All 67

The Lord is Her All in All – Reflections ...68

Friend 70

Friend – Reflections...................................71

My Secret Place 73

My Secret Place – Reflections...................74

How Many?...75

How Many? – Reflections 77

God Is Faithful 78

F.A.I.T.H. 79

Faith – Reflections 80

You Are Not Alone..82

You Are Not Alone – Reflections 83

Father, I Come to You 84

Father, I Come to You – Reflections.........85

God Will Always Be There 87

God Will Always Be There – Reflections .89

God's Master Plan 91

God's Master Plan – Reflections..............93

Highest Ground 94

Highest Ground – Reflections 95

Vision..96

Vision – Reflections 97

Steadfast and True...98

Steadfast and True – Reflections 99

If You Will Believe 100

If You Will Believe – Reflections............101

My Peace...104

God's Love...105

God's Love – Reflections 106

His Song 107

His Song – Reflections 108

More of You, Lord 109

More of You, Lord – Reflections............110

Song In My Heart....................................111

Song in My Heart – Reflections..............112

Broken 113

Broken – Reflections 115

Time...116

Time – Reflections 117

Brand New 119

Brand New – Reflections.........................120

Author's Bio 122

Other Books by Lorraine McCray Castle 123

The Altar Will Alter You

Psalm 43:4 "Then will I go unto the altar of God, unto God my exceeding joy: yea, upon the harp will I praise thee, O God my God."

Lorraine M. Castle

The Altar Will Alter You

The altar will alter the way you look at life.
The altar will alter the way you handle strife.
The altar will strengthen you
and prepare you for the fight.
The altar will alter you.

Jesus waits for you at the altar.
Jesus wants to take you in.
Jesus waits for you at the altar.
At the altar is where new life begins.

Matthew 5:24 — *"Leave there thy gift before the altar, and go thy way; first be reconciled to thy brother, and then come and offer thy gift."*

The Altar Will Alter You

The Altar Will Alter You – Reflections

According to Webster, the definition of alter is, "to make different in some particular, as size, style, course, or the like; modify." Alter represents a definitive change.

Had it not been for Jesus saving me, this book would not have been written. Even though I've written for as long as I can remember, I didn't become a Christian writer until after I rededicated my life to the Lord. With the exception of school assignments most of my writing was personal and had not been shared with anyone other than a card or two that may have been shared with family or close friends.

I'm reminded of my opinion of bumper stickers. Until I was saved, I refused to place a bumper sticker on my car. The first bumper sticker placed on my car read, "God is Good." My mindset regarding bumper stickers was until I was saved, I had nothing to say. The same can be said for what I'm writing today.

When Jesus touched my soul and when I finally accepted His invitation, He gave me a new vocabulary. Suddenly I had plenty to say in the form of Christian poetry, Christian skits, Christian plays, and Christian writing in general. I am compelled to tell the world about His goodness. Today I have plenty to say about my walk with Jesus. The altar truly altered my life!

Heavenly Father, thank you for your patience. While I wandered in the wilderness lost and

3

confused, you never left my side. You offered gentle encouragement even when I didn't know who you were. Thank you for saving me. Amen.

My Deliverer

Psalm 18:17 "He delivered me from my strong enemy, and from them which hated me: for they were too strong for me."

Lorraine M. Castle

I Will Give You Praise

I will give You praise
For the rest of my days
Lord, I adore You.

I will lift You up.
I'll never put You down.
You are my everything.

When I need You,
You are right there by my side.

And You'll lead me
In the midst of my storm,
You're there to be my guide.

And I will give You praise.
For the rest of my days.

John 15:11 – *"These things have I spoken unto you, that my joy might remain in you, and that your joy might be full."*

The Altar Will Alter You

I Will Give You Praise – Reflections

The psalmist said that even 10,000 tongues would not be enough to tell of God's goodness. God just wants us to follow His commandments and give Him all of the praise and glory. That seems like such a simple request, but how often are we taking God's name in vain? Oftentimes when something negative occurs, God's name is the first name to cross our lips.

Negative situations will occur. It's part of life. It cannot be avoided. What is important is how we react to those negative situations. Additionally, we must be mindful that others are looking to us for direction. We are not unique in that respect. Just as we look to others for direction and confirmation, someone is looking to us to teach them by our actions how they should carry themselves when they face adversity.

No matter how bad a situation may be, any day on this side of Heaven is a good day. It's another day that God gave us – another opportunity to give Him all of the praise. My prayer is that more praises will continue to flow from my lips. It's the least that I can do for all He's done for me.

I know I've said it a hundred times, but Lord, I do not have enough breath in my lungs to thank you for everything that you've done in my life and everything that you're going to do in my life. You've placed a joy in my heart that nothing on this earth can replicate. I will give you praise all the rest of my days. Amen.

Lorraine M. Castle

Long Ago on Calvary

Where would I be
Had You not died for me?
Had You not hung on that tree
Long ago on Calvary?

My soul would still be lost
Had You not been willing to pay the cost
To wash my sins away,
You paid a price I could not pay.

You took my pain and made it Your Own.
You never murmured, nor did You groan.
You internalized my sin.
And cleansed me from within
Long ago on Calvary.

Because You've set me free,
I'll serve You through eternity.
It's the least that I can do
To show my gratitude to You.

Where would I be
Had You not died for me?
Had You not hung on that tree
Long ago on Calvary?

II Corinthians 5:17 – *"Therefore if any man be in Christ, he is a new creature: old things are passed away; behold, all things are become new."*

The Altar Will Alter You

Long Ago on Calvary – Reflections

It was Easter morning, 1999. As a member of a growing church congregation then located in Somerdale, NJ, having Easter church service at our church was not going to happen. On a "normal" Sunday, we had three church services – 7:30am, 9:30am, and 11:30am. Each service was packed to capacity. The only building that would hold us on a day such as this was the local civic center.

As I drove the 30 or 40 minutes to the civic center on this calm, sun-shiny Easter Sunday morning, my thoughts went back 2,000 years to the crucifixion of our Lord and Savior, Jesus Christ.

Where would I be had He not died for me? I know I was headed to hell until Jesus touched me in a way I had never before been touched. I was lost, but I didn't know I was lost. I was blind even though I thought I could see where I was headed. I was imprisoned in a bottomless pit that had no beginning and no end. I needed Jesus, but I didn't know I needed Jesus.

Where would I be had He not died for me? I have no clue. What I do know is that I don't want to find out where I would be if there were no Calvary and no sacrifice. Jesus paid a price that we would never be able to pay. He died so that we could live. He saved us. He saved me. And if you let Him, He will save you.

Jesus, thank you for taking me into your bosom.
Thank you for rescuing me from the pits of hell. I
don't want to spend another second away from you.

Lorraine M. Castle

I don't want to think about life without you. Thank you for saving me. Amen.

The Altar Will Alter You

Commissioned

Can you see what I see?
Can you feel what I feel?
In a world plagued with sin,
Can this all be for real?

Souls are lost in despair.
Is there one who will care?
Is there one who can see
We must answer this plea?

We've been commissioned
By a God who cannot fail.
We've been commissioned
Through His power, we will prevail.
We've been commissioned.
Commissioned to do God's will.

Can you see what I see?
Can you hear what I hear?
Souls are crying in pain.
Souls are drowning in fear.
In the midst of their strife,
You can show them new life.
You must show them the way
To our Savior today.

We've been commissioned
By a God who cannot fail.
We've been commissioned
Through His power, we will prevail.
We've been commissioned.
Commissioned to do God's will.

Can you see what I see?

Lorraine M. Castle

Matthew 28:19 – *"Go ye therefore, and teach all nations, baptizing them in the name of the Father, and of the Son, and of the Holy Ghost."*

The Altar Will Alter You

Commissioned – Reflections

"Commissioned" was a personal plea to my heart from the Lord. The Lord does not make a habit of giving a word to us for someone else. God will give us a word that is meant to minister to us first and to others later.

It was late evening and I was unable to sleep. For me, that is generally a "sign" that the Lord has something that He wants to share with me. I'm stubborn and it generally takes several tries before the Lord gets my attention. As I sat in bed waiting for sleep to overtake me, I reached past my Bible to a book by inspirational Christian authors. This book was often comforting to me. I purposely selected a short story that I thought would relax me enough to go to sleep. Today, I could not tell you the name or the author of the short story. What happened next took my full attention.

In the middle of this uplifting and inspiring story, I began to cry. I cried as if my heart were breaking. I could not control the tears. I was soon shivering and lost in my own emotions. In the "background," I could hear myself asking myself, "Why are you crying? You were reading a 'happy' story. Why are you crying?" My answer came from the Lord who answered my question with a question. "Can you see what I see? Can you feel what I feel?" He asked.

I looked up and I saw faces – so many faces. The faces showed anguish, fear, torture and pain. The faces were crying out for help. The Lord spoke again, "These are *my* children! They are hurting.

They are in pain. You must help them. And, you must get others to help them." I cried out, "Lord, I can't do that! How can I help them?!?" The Lord responded ever so softly, "You *can* help them because I will be there every step of the way. I will help you to help my children."

As the Lord commissioned me on that late evening, so did He commission all of us to carry His Gospel to the four corners of the earth spreading His Gospel to every ear that can hear and every eye that can see. All of us have been commissioned to share the Greatness of God!

The bigger question is "How?" How can we take on an assignment such as this? The answer is, "Each one, reach one." Don't wait for someone else because each of us has been commissioned and we can share the goodness of Jesus one person at a time.

Do *you* see what I see?

Lord, first I want to thank you for placing people in my life who taught me about who you are. I want to thank you for helping me to understand your commission so that your truth can be spread to the four corners of the earth. Amen.

The Altar Will Alter You

No Matter

What do you do when you don't want to hear?
What do you do when from God
you've turned your ear?
Where do you run when there's nowhere to hide?
No matter how low
No matter how high
God's been right by your side.

How can you run when He's
kept you from all harm?
How can you hide when He's
 brought you through your storms?
He's been there for you though to Him
you would not turn.
No matter how low
No matter how high
His love for you still burns.

He gave His life to save your soul.
He'll cleanse your heart and make you whole.
No good thing will He withhold.
No matter how low
No matter how high
Let God's Love take control.

Psalm 139:8 – *"If I ascend up into heaven, thou
art there: if I make my bed in hell, behold, thou art
there."*

Lorraine M. Castle

No Matter – Reflections

Have you ever turned a deaf ear to God when you didn't want to hear what he had to say? I'm sorry to say that there have been times when I have turned away after I heard something from God that I didn't want to hear.

I'm reminded of the time when the Holy Spirit directed me to join the Drama Ministry at my church. Anyone who knows me knows that I do not enjoy it when I'm in front of an audience. I'm definitely a behind-the-scenes person. When the Lord spoke to me about joining the Drama Ministry, I ignored Him. I allowed fear of the unknown to direct my path.

The Ministry met on Tuesday evenings. One Tuesday evening I settled in at home after a hard day at work. I clearly heard the Holy Spirit once again instruct me to go to the Drama Ministry meeting. I responded, "Not now," to which the Holy Spirit responded, "If not now, when?" I was startled by the clarity of the question so much so that I went directly to the Drama Ministry meeting. Shortly after arriving, I realized that the Drama Ministry had a writing team! Writing was and still is my heart. It took some prodding on the part of the Holy Spirit, but I am so glad that I answered the Call (eventually).

I certainly understood how Jonah must have felt. "Lord, you want me to do what? You want me to go where?" Jonah preferred to run rather than follow God's command (Book of Jonah – KJV), but as Jonah and many of us found out, we cannot outrun

The Altar Will Alter You

God. In the midst of our sin and disobedience, God is faithful and shows that if we repent, He will save us and protect us. Trust God!

Jesus, thank you for your patience. Thank you for knowing my needs even when I don't know or understand them myself. Thank you for not giving up on me – even when I've appeared to give up on myself. Thank you for your faithfulness. Amen.

Lorraine M. Castle

Temporal Things, Eternal Treasures

When I was small, I had big dreams of owning
many things.

A brand new car, a brand new house, new clothes
and golden rings.

I knew when I acquired _these_ things, I would be a
success.

I'd entertain for all my "friends" to share my
happiness.

I planned it all, achieved it all, when much to my
surprise,

My dreams began to crumble right before my very
eyes.

I lost the car. I lost the house. I managed to keep
the rings.

But, how was I to survive without _all_ of my things?

And, then I heard a voice within say, "Child, I am
the Way.

All the riches in Glory will be yours if you follow
Me today.

The things you lost had become your god. You
were serving them, not Me.

The wages of sin is death, My child. Follow Me to
Eternity.

The Altar Will Alter You

I am the Way, the Truth and the Life. Heaven cannot be gained but by Me.

Material things are not important, My child. Follow Me to Eternity."

Today, I follow Jesus. I grow closer to Him every day.

He instructs me on each step I take. He's leading me all the way.

He strengthens me. He encourages me. I now have the victory.

And I will follow Him all of my days from here to Eternity.

II Corinthians 4:18b – *"...the things which are seen are temporal; but the things which are not seen are eternal."*

Lorraine M. Castle

Temporal Things – Eternal Treasures – Reflections

This is my story. Not unlike many of us, my measurement of success and happiness was based on material things. I began to gather things as soon as I had an income. I had so many things that when I moved from an apartment into a house, the house was filled immediately. While collecting these meaningless possessions, I gave little thought to giving thanks to God or anyone else, for that matter. My belief was that I worked hard for those things and I certainly deserved them!

The danger of my lifestyle is that I was not a "bad" girl. I worked hard on my job. I generally kept a part-time job. I saved my money to attain the material things that I wanted. The problem was that there was no place in my life for God. I had turned from the church 20 years earlier because I made the mistake of equating the people in the church with the church. When I became disillusioned with people, I left the church.

I thank God that I had a praying mother, grandmother, and great-grandmother. There is no other explanation for the turn of events in my life. These ladies held me up through Christ Jesus when I strayed from the church.

When things started to go south in my life, I didn't turn to Jesus. In my warped mind, since I didn't turn to Jesus during the good times, I had no right to reach out to Him now that I realized I needed Him. I can tell you with certainty that thought process is the seed planted by the enemy.

Finding myself in a situation that I could not resolve, I prayed to God and He heard me! Can you imagine that? I left the church for twenty years and He still heard me! God is faithful!

Lord, thank you for your faithfulness. I don't deserve your kindness. There's no way I can earn your faithfulness. All I can do is lean on your word and know that you will never leave me or forsake me. Amen.

Lorraine M. Castle

Who Will You Choose?

Today I have a choice
Because God has given me a voice
To praise His Holy Name
Or take His name in vain.

I can use my two hands to lift Him up
Or my actions can lead another closer
To the path that will corrupt.

I can use my arms to hug someone who's in pain
And filled with despair
Or I can wave that soul away
Without so much as a care.

I can use my feet
To lead a soul to Christ
Or I can trip my brother with a harsh word
That is designed to destroy a life.

Today I have a choice
Because God has given me a voice
To praise His Holy Name
Or take His name in vain.

Who will you choose?

Joshua 24:15 *"...Choose you this day whom ye will serve..."*

The Altar Will Alter You

Who Will You Choose? – Reflections

Everything in life that we do or don't do is the result of a choice. There is an action associated with every reaction. There is a consequence to every decision. One word spoken in haste and in anger can destroy a relationship or send another over the edge. As a child, I learned that "sticks and stones can break my bones, but words can never hurt me." That phrase sounded good, but in actuality, words can and do hurt. The pain inflicted by a harsh word often takes longer to heal than a broken bone. Words from the past can come back to haunt us at the most inopportune moments. Memories of words spoken in anger can freeze us in our tracks. Hurtful words can become the mortar for walls that we have built around us to protect us from the pain. While we cannot undo or rewrite the past, we can address the present and the future. We have choices. We can choose to build up or we can choose to destroy. Which will you choose?

Heavenly Father, I thank you for choices. I thank you for teaching us through your word how you want us to treat our brothers and sisters. I thank you for second chances. While we cannot change or rewrite the past, we have the power to affect the present and the future. Thank you for choices. Amen.

Lorraine M. Castle

Even So

Even though I don't deserve what He has done for
me.
Even though I cannot pay the price He paid for me.
Even though He gave His life for a sinner such as
me.
Even so, He loves me still. Even so.

I turned away.
And He waited.
Patiently for my return.

I am His child.
Through tears He smiled.
When I rushed back to His arms.

Even though I don't deserve what He has done for
me.
Even though I cannot pay the price He paid for me.
Even though He gave His life for a sinner such as
me.
Even so, He loves me still. Even so.

He gave His life on Calvary.
To save a wretched soul like me.
My life was dark and full of sin.
'Til Jesus drew me close Him.

I follow Jesus Christ today.
Because He's showing me the Way.
To live my life in victory.
And then, He's coming back for me.

The Altar Will Alter You

Deuteronomy 4:31 – *"He will not forsake thee, neither destroy thee, nor forget the covenant of thy fathers which he sware unto them."*

Lorraine M. Castle

Even So – Reflections

Do you know that God loves you even when you turn your back on Him? I turned my back on the church for nearly 20 years. I was confused. I travelled in a never-ending circle as I searched to fill a void that could not be filled. During my struggle, there was a voice within me that from time-to-time would beckon me to follow. It was a soft-spoken, comforting voice, but I would not answer the call. Today, I realize that voice was the Holy Spirit calling me to come home.

Those of us who have turned our backs on God did so for numerous reasons. I'm here to tell you that it's never too late to return to your first love. He is there waiting for you. He will not turn His back on you. He will never turn you away. You will not be rejected. He's loved you through your good and your bad times.

When I turned my back on God, I had the mindset that I would return to Him when I got myself together. There was a time when I didn't care for friends who reached out to me only when things were in a dire state for them. It's not that I didn't want to help them, but I believed they should have reached out in good times rather than waiting until the situation was urgent.

I thought God felt the same way about us. I forgot that our ways are not His ways and our thoughts are not His thoughts (Isaiah 55:8-9). We cannot fix ourselves. If we could, we would have already done so (Bishop David G. Evans). God will take us just

The Altar Will Alter You

as we are. He will mold us and heal us. He will make us brand new.

Even though you may have done what you or others consider the worse sin imaginable, Jesus is waiting for you with open arms. Run to Him now!

Lord, I don't even know where to begin. You loved me when I did not love myself. You held your hand out to me when I turned my back to you. You are a God of second, third, and fourth chances. Thank you for being there for me. Amen.

Lorraine M. Castle

God's Time

There was a time
When I took the time
To listen to the birds chirping in the morning.
I loved to hear them praising the Lord in a way that
only they can praise Him.

There was a time
When I took the time
To go for a walk early in the morning
It was just me and the Lord and His Kingdom that
He created just for us.

There was a time
When I took the time
To count the stars in the clear evening sky
To watch an airplane flying in the distance and
wonder where it was headed
To smell the sweet evening air
And feel the cool evening breeze as it tickled my
eyelashes

There was a time
When I took the time
To enjoy and marvel over the wonders of the earth
That God has freely given all of us

There was a time
When I took the time
But…. Now… I have… No Time.

John 9:4 – *"I must work the works of him that sent
me, while it is day: the night cometh, when no man
can work."*

The Altar Will Alter You

God's Time. – Reflections

We know we must work while it's day. We know that time has its limitations. While we are busily working to complete that which we've been ordained to do in the name of the Lord, we cannot forget to take time to spend time with our Creator. God desires that we spend time with Him. It's during this time that He speaks to us and pours into us. Just as we require quite time with our loved ones, God wants us to spend some quiet time with Him. When we talk to God, allow time to listen for His response. We must make time for His Time.

Lord Jesus, my Father in Heaven, thank you for being there for me at all times. You are never too busy to listen to my concerns. Help me to give you the quality time that you deserve. Thank you. Amen.

Lorraine M. Castle

Sister, Sister

Sister, Sister – You don't need that mister.

I know he can treat you like a queen –
when he wants to

I know you think he's the man of your dreams –
when he wants to be

But, then he can turn on you faster
than you can turn the page
of the next chapter in your life.

He can erase
That smitten smile from your face –
Faster than you can –

Wipe the scent of his cologne from your hands –
Faster than you can wipe the tears from your eyes
Tears fueled by his lies…

Sister, Sister – You don't need that mister.

I know you fear the loneliness
more than you fear the heartache

I know you fear the empty nights
more than you fear his empty promises

I know you fear spending the rest of your days
alone

But, Sister, Sister – You really don't need that
mister.

The Altar Will Alter You

He's putting you down
in a vain attempt to lift himself up.

He's inflicting pain to ease his
discomfort and disappointment.

He's trying to squash the life out of you,

But, just as a grape must be crushed
to appreciate the essence that dwells within

My prayer is that you will allow your essence
to flow and realize that

Sister, Sister – You don't need that mister.

Allow a new man to enter your life.
Let me introduce you to the Man from Jericho.

Let me introduce you to the Man
who can truly set you free.

The man who knows you better
than you know yourself.

The man who has known you
since before you were conceived.

The man who will teach you what
it really is to be loved by a man.

Let Jesus teach you about real love.
Unconditional love.
You know, that love that
you think you're unworthy of.

Lorraine M. Castle

That love that makes your backbone slip.
That love that puts the quiver in your lip.

That love you thought was just in fairy tales.
That love that will make a grown man wail.
That love from Jesus that will never fail.
Let me introduce you to the air in your sail.

Sister, Sister, now that's the Mister.

He'll lift you up and cleanse you from the inside out
He'll show you what love's all about.

And, once you know what love is,
You'll know what love ain't!

You'll know it ain't
the missed birthdays and anniversaries.
You'll know it ain't pain, grief or heartache.
You'll know it ain't what you've been getting.
And, then…

Sister, Sister – You'll drop that old mister

And you'll wait –
For real love.

Psalm 37:23 – *"The steps of a good man are
ordered by the Lord: and he delighteth in his way."*

The Altar Will Alter You

Sister, Sister – Reflections

We were created to be loved. John 3:16 teaches us that God loved us so much that He gave His Son to save us from our sins. Love doesn't hurt. Love is not telling me that you love me and then hurting me as only a loved one can. Love is showing me that you love me by protecting me from all hurt, harm, and danger. God's word describes the true meaning of love (1st Corinthians 13). Often love is mistaken for material things. At times, we will enter into a relationship simply because we don't want to be alone. We attempt to fill a void with a person.

Only God can fill the void in our soul. Only God can replace that longing with His love. Establishing a relationship with God will prepare your heart for the love of a man or woman. Before turning my life over to the Lord, there was a distinct separation between my relationship with God and my relationships with the opposite sex. God had no place in those relationships. As a result, those relationships did not and could not last. God is the foundation for all relationships.

You are my Lord and Savior. Yet, I didn't invite you into my relationships. Thank you for giving me a chance to invite you into my life. Thank you for showing me true love. Thank you for your Joy, Peace, and Wisdom to recognize your love in others. Amen.

Lorraine M. Castle

The Gift

The Gift is more precious than silver or gold.
It cannot be touched, but it's easy to hold.
It cannot be bought by the richest of men.
But, it can be given to all who seek Him.

Once The Gift has been given, it can't be taken
away.
Although we may stumble. Although we may stray.
We have been purchased and bought with a price.
The Gift from our Saviour is Eternal Life!

Ephesians 2:8 – *"For by grace are ye saved
through faith; and that not of yourselves: it is The
Gift of God."*

The Altar Will Alter You

The Gift – Reflections

Lord, what would we do without your gift? What would we do had you not taken mercy on us and saved us? I cannot even imagine my life without you. The wonderful thing about your gift is that, while you knew I needed you, I didn't know I needed you. The dictionary defines the word "gift" as, "something given voluntarily without payment in return, as to show favor toward someone, honor an occasion, or make a gesture of assistance..." What a perfect definition. The Holy Spirit freely gave of Himself. He showed favor upon us. We could not and cannot earn the gift. But, the gift is freely given to all who declare Jesus as their Savior.

Thank you Jesus for your gift. Thank you for showering us with your Love. Thank you for freely giving us that which could not be purchased or earned. Thank you for Eternal Life. Amen.

My Protector

Psalm 91:4 "He shall cover thee with his feathers, and under his wings shalt thou trust: his truth shall be thy shield and buckler."

Lorraine M. Castle

Your Child is in God's Hands

Your child is in God's hands.
The battle belongs to the Lord.
Allow Him to lift your burden of sorrow
Find comfort in His Word.

Your child is in God's hands.
The Lord will see him through.
He feels alone, but that is not so.
We know this, for God's Word is true.

Your child is in God's hands.
He'll gain the victory through your hope.
The strength of God that shines through you
Will show him that he, too, can cope.

Your child is in God's hands.
He's been there all the long.
The Lord will comfort and strengthen your child.
It's in our weakness that God becomes strong.

Your child is in God's hands.
His life has just begun.
And though the future may now appear dim,
Remember, the battle has already been won!

Your child is in God's hands.
You may wonder when this season will end.
But, in God's Time - and in God's Way,
God will bring your child home again.

The Altar Will Alter You

Proverbs 22:6 – *"Train up a child in the way he should go: and when he is old, he will not depart from it."*

Lorraine M. Castle

Your Child is in God's Hands – Reflections

You've given your child all you had to give. You nurtured him. You protected him. You instructed him with words of wisdom. You introduced him to Jesus Christ early in life… and yet, your child has gone astray. The pain of watching a part of you; someone you knew before he knew himself; someone you cared for and loved before he was even born can only be compared to the pain that our Lord and Savior feels each time one of His own goes astray.

It was this concern that inspired "*Your Child Is In God's Hands*." I don't know a mother's pain intimately. I have no biological children of my own, but I have watched as others watched their legacy appear to fizzle. They had such high hopes. Where did they go wrong as a parent? What could they have done differently? In my imagination's eye, our Father in Heaven has asked this question of Himself, "Why don't my children love Me?"

We were created in the image of our Father. He placed the love of Jesus within the very depths of our soul. It is hidden in our hearts. The love of and for Jesus is the purest love of all. The love of Jesus is unconditional. It cannot be earned and it is not warranted. While man has been created in the image of God, man has a will of his own. It is this will that allows us to choose God or choose the world.

Since we don't deserve the love of God, it's difficult to understand His unconditional love. There is nothing on earth to compare with the love of God.

The Altar Will Alter You

We search for artificial means of the love of God in the world. We're comfortable with the things of the world. Unlike God whom we have never physically seen, we know the world. We were born into the world. We look for that which we were born into to provide that which we are seeking.

As Jesus is the Light; so is the world darkness. Darkness seeks out darkness in drugs, alcohol, and other addictive venues. The things of the world are artificial and fruitless. The search for completeness in the world is unfulfilling and disappointing.

Often we do not return to our First Love until we've reached the bottomless pit that the world offers. We cannot measure the depth of another's pit. My prayer is that each child of God who is ensnarled in the abyss of the world will see that small, yet brilliant light at the end of their tunnel realizing that God can penetrate all forms of darkness. Yes, even in darkness, your child is in God's hands.

Jesus, I am so glad that you can reach us wherever we are. I know that just as you've watched over the sparrow, you have each child of God in the palm of your hand. My prayer is that each parent will be comforted with that knowledge. Amen.

Lorraine M. Castle

We Can Pray

What can we do when we don't know what to do?

We can pray for the souls
of our loved ones who've departed.

We can pray for deliverance
of those who are empty hearted.

If we look to the Lord for Salvation on this day.
We can pray. We can pray.

We can pray for the Lord
hears the prayers of the righteous.

Through the Blood of our Lord,
Holy Spirit do invite us

To commune with our Lord
as we seek His Grace today.

When we pray. We can pray.

Prayer answers things beyond our understanding.
Prayer is the bridge between man and God.
If we look to the Lord for Salvation on this day.
If we seek His face. If we know He is the Way.
If we humble ourselves as we honor God today.
We can pray. We can pray. We can pray.

Matthew 21:22 – *"And all things, whatsoever ye
shall ask in prayer, believing, ye shall receive."*

The Altar Will Alter You

We Can Pray – Reflections

Most of us know exactly what we were doing on the morning of September 11, 2001. Like most of us, I was devastated as I watched the destruction of the Twin Towers. During the days that followed, I was glued to the television screen as I prayed for the lost souls and for the survivors and their families. I asked God what can I do when I don't know what to do? His response to me was that I can pray. While there is always work to be done, we must not place prayer on the back burner. God wants us to seek His face in everything that we do. Proverbs 3:6 says, "In all thy ways acknowledge him, and he shall direct thy paths." We serve an all-powerful, all-loving God and He cares for each one of us.

Prayer is having a conversation with God. God made a point of teaching us how to pray (Matthew 6:9-13) so that we can communicate with Him. Bishop David G. Evans has been teaching us that we do not have to kneel and close our eyes in order to pray and communicate with God. We can pray anywhere at any time – even during a meeting at work. Establishing communication with God through prayer is so important. Leaving time to receive a response from God is a part of prayer. Remember communication is a two-way street.

Thank You, Lord for loving me, caring for me, and answering my prayers. Amen.

Lorraine M. Castle

God Is!

God Is. God Is!

There are not enough nouns, pronouns or adjectives.
There are not enough shades of blue, green, red or
purple.

There are not enough feelings of joy, peace, hope or
contentment
To describe what God is.

So –
Why don't I break *this* down
By first talking about what God is *not*!

God is NOT depression.
Depression is deflated emotions.
God is NOT deflated.

God is NOT heavy.
Heaviness is an unbearable burden.
Heaviness makes a soul weary.
God is NOT weak nor is He weary.

God is NOT a void.
He is NOT darkness.
He is NOT distant.
He is NOT untouchable.
He is NOT corruptible.

God is NOT surprised by what you do
Nor is He surprised by what you don't do.

The Altar Will Alter You

Like not giving tithes.
Telling lies.
Faking alibis.
All this is Sin in His eyes.

As a word to the Wise
Accept what cannot be denied
Because… God Is!

God Is irreplaceable.
He Is irresistible.
God is multifaceted.

He Is all encompassing
God Is like Surround Sound
He's everywhere!
There is nowhere where He is Not!
He's all up in your stuff!
Hide from God?
You can't hide from God
Because… God Is!

He Is the Peace in your storm.
He Is the Blanket that keeps you warm.
He Is your Shield and Protector from all harm.
Yes, God Is!

God Is the "O" in your JOY
Because He's always in the midst.

He's the "B" in your Bless
Because without *His* blessing
You would be *less* than He would have you to be.

He is the "G" in your Grace
Because you need God to run this race!

Lorraine M. Castle

He Is the "A" in your Amen
Because He Is your Alpha and Omega
Your beginning *and* your end!

God Is the GLORY in your Hallelujah!
Yes, God Is!

God Is whatever you need Him to be.
He's whatever you *allow* Him to be.
Submission is the key
To life eternally
Get in God's Word and see
What happens when you let God Be.

Because…. God Is!

Exodus 3:14 – "*And God said unto Moses, I AM THAT I AM…*"

The Altar Will Alter You

God Is! – Reflections

Have you ever tried to explain to someone who God is? Imagine you met someone who had never heard of God and had no concept of God. How would you describe Him? Would you be able to find words that adequately describe Him? If God were a color, what color would he be? There is so much that God is – so much that He encompasses – that initially, it may be easier to describe what God is not.

We know that anything that is not good is not God. God is not depression, oppression, or obsession. God is not a heavy burden. We know that in God, there is fullness of joy; therefore, God is not a void. God is The Light, so we know He is not darkness. While God is not darkness, He can lead us out of darkness. He can fill the void in our lives.

God is not someone or something that you can put away when you enter the dark side and then bring Him out – for example on Sundays – when you want to be in His presence. When God said that He would never leave you or forsake you, that's exactly what He meant. God is there when you want Him to be and He's there when you would prefer that He disappear.

Like the holiday song, "He sees you when you're sleeping. He's there when you're awake..."[1] God is there all of the time. The question is, do you acknowledge His presence. Because God is always there, He's not surprised by what you do and He's

---

[1] **"Santa Claus is Coming to Town" by John Frederick Coots and Haven Gillespie**

not surprised by what you don't do. God has given us free will to follow Him or to make our path.

God wants us to submit to His will. He wants us to do so willingly. He's no different than we are in that respect. We want to be loved, but we don't want to force someone – anyone – to love us. It's the same with God. Submit to His will and you will know for yourself Who God Is.

Lord, I thank you for accepting me as I am. I thank you for giving me the opportunity to live freely within you. I thank you for your patience while you waited for me as I continue to learn day-by-day just who you are. Amen.

The Altar Will Alter You

Jesus Is The Answer

Have you ever felt so lonely
In the midst of a thousand-fold?
Have you ever been surrounded by warmth,
Yet within you all is cold?

Have you ever felt like giving up
In the midst of helping hands?
Jesus is the answer,
And all your pain He will understand.

You have searched within yourself
In hopes that the answer lies therein.
You have searched among your friends
And found disappointments time and again.

You have searched through valleys near and far
And you've found no peace and no rest.
Jesus is the answer
To your peace and your happiness.

Jesus is the answer.
Jesus is the Way.
Jesus is the Answer.
So, won't you call on Him today?

He will fill your life with gladness;
All the joys that you desire.
He'll restore the warmth within your heart
As He sets your soul on fire.

He will lift you up to higher ground
As you glorify His name.
Jesus is the answer
And every day, it will be the same.

Jesus is the answer.
Jesus is the Way.
Jesus is the Answer.
So, won't you call on Him today?

Hebrews 10:23 *"Let us hold fast the profession of our faith without wavering; for He is faithful that promised."*

The Altar Will Alter You

Jesus Is The Answer – Reflections

Have you ever felt lonely even though you were in a room full of people? I know I have. I had a void in my soul. I was popular with people. I've never had to search for friends. But, my life felt empty. I felt like a shell. I was unable to connect with people. Something that I couldn't define was missing from my life.

I had a good job, my own place, a nice car, nice wardrobe and an active social life. These were all of the "things" that the world used as a barometer to one's success. However, inside I felt empty. I felt I had no purpose and no worth. During this period of my life, I also did volunteer work through the American Red Cross where I helped people who had lost all of their belongings because of a fire in their home. I also volunteered through my sorority, Delta Sigma Theta, Inc., at area nursing homes. I was doing all of the "right" things, but I felt I had no purpose.

I've heard people say, "You need Jesus." Although, at times, this sounds like a cliché, it is the truth. I had no church life. I was raised in the church. I was actually saved at the age of 12. I became disenfranchised with the church and left. I returned to the church after being away from it for 20-years.

It was such a sense of relief. When I joined my church, I was in a new area where I had no friends. When I walked into church on that 3rd Sunday in May, I was immediately embraced by the love of Jesus. I realized that after 20 years, I was home! For 20 years, my soul searched for what was missing in my life – I needed Jesus. All of us need Jesus. He is the answer to every asked and unasked question. Yes. Jesus is the answer!

Jesus, thank you for your patience. Thank you for watching over me and caring for me while I looked for you in all the wrong places. I am home, now. Thank you for keeping the door open and the light on for me. Amen.

The Altar Will Alter You

He Is!

He is the Rock of my salvation,
My strength when I can't go on.

He is the understanding Counsel,
My guide when my walk has gone wrong.

He is my Sanctuary,
When trouble comes my way.

He is my sure Foundation,
In Him I cannot stray.

He is my soul (and sole) Provider,
Through Him I can do all things.

He is my strong Tower,
To Him I forever will cling.

He is my Redeemer,
The Son of man and God's Lamb.

He is that He is that He is that He is,
And because He is – I am.

Exodus 3:14 *"...I Am that I Am..."*

Lorraine M. Castle

He Is! – Reflections

There is no one thing on this earth that can fulfill every need. On the other hand, there is no need that Jesus cannot fill. Now, to make sure there's no confusion, there are wants and there are needs. Jesus promised to fulfill our needs. I believe wants fall under a different category. Jesus is looking for a relationship with us.

He wants us to come to Him first. I remember the hymn I sang as a child,

> "Oh, what peace we often forfeit
> Oh, what needless pain we bear
> All because we do not carry
> Everything to God in prayer."[2]

I think of all of the distress I've gone through simply because I didn't follow this simple instruction. Jesus was there waiting for me to come to him. He never wavered. He never strayed. He was intent on being these as soon as I realized I needed Him. Jesus is my everything. I am made in His image. I am a reflection of Him. Therefore, everything I need can be found in Him.

Jesus, you are my everything. There is no me without you. thank you for fulfilling my every need. Amen.

---

[2] **"What a Friend We Have in Jesus" written in 1855 by Joseph M. Scriven (public domain)**

My Provider

Psalm 132:15 "I will abundantly bless her provision: I will satisfy her poor with bread."

Lorraine M. Castle

Christian Friends

We have a friend in Jesus
No better friend has man known.
He leads us and He guides us.
He calls each of us His own.

He promised never to leave us.
He's been there since before our birth.
And in His infinite wisdom,
He's given us Christian friends here on earth.

He's given us friends to help comfort us –
Friends to help wipe away our tears.
He's given us friends to help support us –
Friends to help calm our deepest fears.

He's given us friends to share in our joy –
Friends to help brighten each and every day.
He's given us friends who think it not robbery
To walk the Christian Way.

Yes, Jesus is The Ultimate Friend.
He'll be with us until the end.
And I thank God through Jesus Christ
That you are my Christian friend!

John 15:13 – *"Greater love hath no man than this,
that that a man lay down his life for his friends."*

The Altar Will Alter You

Christian Friends – Reflections

My friend doesn't know it, but he was my first. It was a Saturday afternoon. I spent the morning running errands and I was happy to be home planning how I would spend my Saturday evening at home. Even though I was alone, I wasn't lonely.

It suddenly occurred to me that I neglected to pick up a birthday card that I would need for the next day. It was now late in the evening. Not wanting to go back out, I sat down and began to write my first birthday poem and presented it to my friend the next day in place of a birthday card. For the next year most of my friends received original poetry from me as part of their birthday gift.

It was an unintentional use of my gift. I thank God for the gift of writing and I thank Him for Christian friends who often inspire me to write.

Lord, thank you for allowing me to see the beauty around me. Darkness may abound, but you have given us Christian friends to remind us that we are not alone. I know that you are my ultimate friend, but it is nice to have Christian friends to help me in my walk. Amen.

Lorraine M. Castle

I . C . Z . (Insulated Comfort Zone)

To get with Me
Get out your I.C.Z.
Get out your I.C.Z.
To truly be set free.

To truly be set free
Just face reality.
You've got to let God Be.
Get out your I.C.Z.

God wants to bust a move
So True Love He can prove.
He wants to cleanse your soul
So He can make you whole.

He'll cleanse you from within
And free you from your sin.
He wants you to come home.
Get out your comfort zone!

'Cause once you let God in,
Eternal Life you'll win.
Just lose your I.C.Z.
And get with G.O.D.!

Matthew 16:24 – *"Then said Jesus unto his disciples, If any* man *will come after me, let him deny himself, and take up his cross, and follow me."*

The Altar Will Alter You

I. C. Z. (Insulated Comfort Zone) – Reflections

Jesus said to His disciples, "Follow Me." That sounds like such a simple instruction – and it is. We are disciples. Jesus wants us to follow Him. Often we have our own aspirations and desires. We want to do what we want to do. We are our own persons. How quickly we forget, "...*seek ye first* the kingdom of God, and his righteousness; and all these things shall be added unto you." (Matthew 6:33) When we put God first, everything else will fall into place.

Lord, Jesus, you have given us the formula for success in all areas of our life. One simple instruction – Follow Me. You are so generous. For following this simple instruction, you will give us the desires of our heart. Thank you for everything that you're doing in my life. Amen.

Lorraine M. Castle

Precious

Can you serve My precious children?
Can you guide them on their way?
Can you listen when they cry out?
Can you teach them how to pray?

Can you share their precious moments?
Can you calm their deepest fears?
Can you be there when they call out?
Can you dry their weeping tears?

Can you teach My precious children
In the way that they should go?
Can you be their walking Bible?
Can you teach them all you know

About my Beloved Son, Jesus
Who died to set them free?
He is their soul salvation.
Can you teach them these things for Me?

You are My chosen vessel.
I chose you to do My Will.
I chose you to lead My children.
I chose you to serve until

My children come to know Me
Through the example you have shown.
They will know that I'm their Father
Through the seeds that you have sown.

They will know they have a destiny.
They will know that on this earth
Each child will serve My purpose
That was assigned before their birth.

The Altar Will Alter You

Continue to lead My precious children
Until that destined day
When we meet in the hereafter,
I will look at you and say,

"Well done My good and faithful servant.
I am pleased with all you have done.
Precious child, enter into the Kingdom
Of your Father, Holy Ghost and My Son."

Proverbs 22:6 – *"Train up a child in the way he should go: and when he is old he will not depart from it."*

Lorraine M. Castle

Precious – Reflections

It was a mission – an assignment thrust upon me. It was an upcoming celebration of appreciation honoring our Youth Minister and I was asked to write a skit or a poem as a gift from the Drama Ministry to our Youth Minister. I humbly accepted the task and immediately panicked as every single thought immediately vanished from my brain and I was left with muddled nothingness that had to be transformed into something meaningful. To add to the level of stress, it was decided that the skit or poem would be recited in conjunction with a mime performance. No pressure.

I continually praise God for the way He shows up and shows out! I struggled for the right words. I spent hours staring at a blank piece of paper willing my mind to be creative! I walked. I prayed. I listened to music. I prayed. I listened to stark silence. I prayed. I prayed. I prayed. The Holy Spirit spoke softly. My soul embraced the words. "Tell him to take care of my precious children."

The words flowed into my spirit. My fingers flew across my computer keyboard as I attempted to capture every word. Words, phrases, and letters tumbled from my spirit jockeying for position on paper, willing my words to be presented in the proper order and in proper order.

Words that had never been spoken in just this manner introduced themselves to my fingers and established a relationship with paper. These words, while written for our Youth Minister are intended for everyone. We have been charged with taking

The Altar Will Alter You

care of God's children – young, old, and of every nationality. All of God's children are precious.

Lord, thank you for allowing me to be your vessel. Thank you for pouring into my spirit so that I can pour into the souls of others. Thank you for loving me and encouraging me. There is nothing that I can do; nor is there anything that I would want to do without you. Amen.

Lorraine M. Castle

Christian Hospitality

I felt the love and warmth of God
As soon as I walked in.
God's presence shown around about,
His Spirit dwelled therein.

You treated me like royalty
Because I am His child.
Your spirit was so humble,
Your mannerism so mild.

I thank God because you allow Him
To continue a work through you.
And I pray that your love for others
Will continue to bring love back to you!

Romans 12:10 – *"Be kindly affectioned one to another with brotherly love, in honor referring one another."*

The Altar Will Alter You

Christian Hospitality – Reflections

Lord, I know that you are our Friend, our Protector, our Comforter, our All-in-All. It is so wonderful that while you are our everything, you realize that we also have a need for friends here on earth. I thank you that you have surrounded us with others who love you as much as we love you. We're surrounded with others who are like-minded and headed in the same direction. We're able to fellowship and celebrate your grace and your mercy.

Lord, we thank you for Christian hospitality. We thank you for surrounding us with people who love, honor, and serve you. We know that you are there for us and that you will never leave us. We are grateful for Christian hospitality. Amen.

Lorraine M. Castle

The Lord is Her All in All

She walks upright when she enters a room.
Her stature, sure-footed and tall.
She's so full of grace
When she enters a place.
The Lord is her all in all.

She remains calm in the eye of a storm.
She stands still when life throws a curveball.
Why is she so cool
When confusion appears to rule?
The Lord is her all in all.

She speaks words of wisdom
when others are at a loss.
She sees a door where others see a wall.
From whence comes her vision
When others suffer indecision?
The Lord is her all in all.

She knows that the Lord
will keep her safe and warm.
She knows that the Lord
will protect her from all harm.
She knows that the Lord will never let her fall.
The Lord is her all in all.

Psalm 23:1 – *"The Lord is my shepherd; I shall not want."*

The Altar Will Alter You

The Lord is Her All in All – Reflections

Psalm 37:4 teaches us that if we "take delight in the Lord...he will give you the desires of your heart." (NIV) Matthew 6:33 tells us to "...seek first the kingdom of God and his righteousness, and all these things will be added to you." (ESV) All we have to do is put God first in all things. That sounds reasonable enough. However, it can be a continuous tug-of-war because man (or woman) wants to be the boss.

We like to do things our way in our own time. If we've lived long enough, we discover that our way often is not the best way. We see our situation with tunnel vision from our perspective only. God sees the entire picture. He created us, so He knows what is best for us. Keeping your ear inclined to Him allows you to follow His directive. Doing so allows you to walk with assured confidence.

As a child, I learned by observing others. As an adult, I continue to learn people by observing them. My Pastor has a favorite saying, "Don't tell me you love me, show me you love me." That phrase is so true. Have you ever had someone say something harsh to you and then have them say, "I was only kidding." Did that statement ease the initial pain that was felt when the statement was made? I think not.

We never know who may be watching us and molding their actions and responses after our own. A person that comes to mind is a member of my church. She was a minister. I never met her personally (my church has 27,000 members), but I loved to watch her praise the Lord. She became ill, but she continued to work in the church and her praise was not diminished. Her body became frail, but she continued to praise the Lord because The Lord Was Her All In All. Several months after she passed away, I became ill. During my illness, I never lost my joy. This minister's actions taught me how to keep my joy by praising the Lord in good times and in bad times.

Romans 8:28 says all things are working together because you are walking in His footsteps. What a wonderful place to be when the Lord Is Your All In All.

My Father in Heaven, thank You for being my all in all. Everything I need is found in you. I am surrounded by your love. You are my shelter, protector, doctor, lawyer, mother, father. You are my everything. My all in all. Amen.

The Altar Will Alter You

Friend

Lord, You are my Friend.
You are the Joy of my salvation.
You're the Healer of my soul.
And to You I give control
Of my heart, my mind, my life.

Because You are my Friend.
You are my Strength when I am weary.
You're the reason why I sing.
Lord, You are my everything.

You are my Hope.
You are my Peace.
Lord, You are my Friend!

John 15:13 – *"Greater love hath no man than this, that a man lay down His life for His friends."*

Lorraine M. Castle

Friend – Reflections

Every friend has his or her limit. They may proclaim that they will do anything and go anywhere for a friend and that may be true – to an extent. Every friendship has a limit. No one is expected to put him or herself in harm's way to save a friend, but some of us have been blessed with a friend or friends who have sacrificed their life to save a friend – even to save the life of someone they don't know. We call them heroes.

Would that friend sacrifice his or her life time and time again? Would that friend stand up for us even when the evidence clearly indicates that we are guilty? The friend we have in Jesus will do that for each and every one of us every day if only we ask Him.

Psalm 46:1 tells us that God is our refuge and our strength – a present help in time of trouble. This tells me that whenever I'm in trouble, God will be there for me. I don't have to wait for office hours or even make an appointment. He is there for me. Period.

God has no limitations or boundaries. He will be our friend, our mother, father, sister, or brother. He will fill whatever void we allow Him to fill. He is truly our everything. There is no need that He cannot fulfill. He is the answer to the unasked question – the destination to the undetermined journey. He completes us. All that is required is the personalized invitation from us.

The Altar Will Alter You

Thank you, Jesus, for being my friend. Thank you for supplying all of my needs. I thank you for accepting me in my unfinished state. I thank you for leading and guiding my steps. Amen.

Lorraine M. Castle

My Secret Place

I have a secret place
Where I will sometimes flee.
It's a place that's kept well hidden
So others cannot see.

My secret is the part of me
That I have not released
To my Lord and Savior, Jesus Christ,
My King and Prince of Peace.

Why do I hold on to this place?
When I know yielding will erase
The pain that daily I must face?
And, yet, I return to my secret place.

Psalm 139:7 – *"Whither shall I go from thy spirit?
or whither shall I flee from thy presence?"*

The Altar Will Alter You

My Secret Place – Reflections

I'm certain I wouldn't be alone if I admitted that even though I've sung "I Surrender All" at the top of my lungs and professed how much I love the Lord, there is still a small part of my heart that I've reserved for myself. I know this is selfish – especially when I know that yielding 100% will remove any remaining anxieties I have about this thing that we call life.

It boggles my mind that I have not surrendered all to Jesus. Yet, I know that I am not alone. Knowing I'm not alone is no consolation. In my mind, I know that there is no need to withhold anything from Jesus. He wants only the best for me. He gave His life for me! In my heart, that is weakened by the cruelty of this world, I guard against the ultimate hurt that would surely kill me.

My prayer is that I will learn to trust God more and more each day. I'll take baby steps surrendering a little more every day. As stated so eloquently in the hymn, "Oh for grace to trust Him more.[3]"

Dearest Jesus, thank you for forgiving me for not trusting you 100%. I pray that each day I grow closer to you leaving behind me the familiar things of the world. Amen.

---

[3] **From the hymn "Tis So Sweet to Trust in Jesus" composer – Louisa M. R. Stead (1850-1917) – Public Domain**

Lorraine M. Castle

How Many?

How many drops of water
are there in a stream?

How many realities are caught up in a dream?
How many times on Him
will Christ allow us to lean?
How many?

How many times will we stumble and not fall?
How many times on the name of Jesus will we call?
How many times will Jesus show us
He is our All in All?
How many?

How many times from Jesus will we stray?
How many times will we try to walk away?
How many times
before we realize that His is the only Way?
How many?

How many times will God illustrate His love?
How many times will God look on us from above?
While He continues to keep us
wrapped up in His love?
How many?

Ten thousand times the drops in a stream.
Ten thousand times your mended dreams.
Ten thousand times ten thousand times
    the largest number you've ever seen...
How many times? That's how many.

The Altar Will Alter You

1st John 1:9 – *"If we confess our sins, he is faithful and just to forgive us [our] sins, and to cleanse us from all unrighteousness."*

Lorraine M. Castle

How Many? – Reflections

"If at first you don't succeed, try, try again." How many times have we heard this? How many times have we fallen? It doesn't matter how many times we've fallen. What matters is that we get up, dust ourselves off, and begin again. A failure is not a failure until or unless we stop trying. God does not see us as failures. He sees us a works in progress. We are made in God's image. God cannot fail; therefore, God does not expect us to fail. He wants us to trust in Him enough to know that if He says it is so, then it is so.

Jesus. Jesus. Jesus. Thank you for being my Savior. Thank you for casting my sins into the sea of forgetfulness. Thank you for being an ever-loving God. Amen.

God Is Faithful

1st Corinthians 1:9 "God is faithful, by whom ye were called unto the fellowship of his Son Jesus Christ our Lord."

Lorraine M. Castle

F.A.I.T.H.

F   Forge ahead and be not weary. The battle is not yours; it's the Lord's.

A   Always keep your eye on the Prize. Heavenly places will be your reward.

I   Irrespective of how the future may look, things are not always as they appear.

T   Trust in the Lord to carry your burdens. He'll be there for you – never fear.

H   Harken to The Word of our Lord and Savior. He will never lead you astray.

Have FAITH that He Who has brought you this far will continue to show you   His Way.

II Corinthians 5:7 – *"For we walk by faith, not by sight."*

The Altar Will Alter You

Faith – Reflections

Faith. This is the area where many Christians – myself included – struggle. So important is faith that a version of the word "faith" appears in the King James Version of The Bible 336 times. Hebrews 11:6 tells us that without faith we cannot please God. We want to please God. I want to please God, but how can I please God when my faith waivers?

God gave me the answer in the poem, *"Faith."* Faith is the evidence of things not seen. I don't have to see what's beyond. I just need to press on. The battle isn't mine. It's the Lord's (II Chronicles 20:15). I must persevere keeping my mind on the goal.

The opportunity to exercise our faith presents itself when we are faced with obstacles. Just as we must exercise in order to keep our bodies in shape, we must exercise our faith so that it can be strengthened.

When we're struggling with keeping the faith, remember what God has already done in your life. Look at what He's done for others. God loves all of us with the same measure. What He has done for others He will do for you. Faith *is* the evidence of things unseen. Faith is not based on what we see. It may not look like you want it to look. Have faith "that he which hath begun a good work in you will perform it until the day of Jesus Christ." (Philippians 1:6)

Lorraine M. Castle

How many times have we given up just shy of reaching our goal? We don't know the end. We only know that in the end, we win. So, don't give up. Press forward. Keep the faith!

Heavenly Father, I ask you to help my unbelief. Help me to stay focused on you when chaos erupts. Help me to remember that you are with me every step of the way. When I am feeling alone and isolated, you are there. When others forsake me and speak poorly of me, you are there. Please remind me to keep the faith even in my darkest hours. Amen.

The Altar Will Alter You

You Are Not Alone

I cannot know the depths of your grief.
I cannot know your pain.
I cannot know how bleak the future looks
As you realize life will not be the same.

But, Who I know is a Savior
Who hears your every cry.
He'll relieve your burdens one by one.
He'll wipe that tear from your eye.

He promised never to leave you.
He promised He'd always be there.
You have only to seek the Master.
He will hear your humble prayer.

He'll give you the strength you need to endure.
He'll give you peace of mind.
He'll give you comfort through the endless nights.
A solace you will find.

Just trust in His Word and His Promise.
And know that this, too, shall pass.
And know that the loved one you're missing
Is resting in peace at last.

John 14:18 – *"I will not leave you comfortless: I will come to you."*

Lorraine M. Castle

You Are Not Alone – Reflections

Losing a loved one to death creates a void that cannot be filled. We try to comfort each other during this difficult time, but the reality is that your life has been changed forever. Your loved one is gone from this earth and you are left here to carry on. You feel that you've been deserted. Even though you know that your loved one is in a better place, your heart is a slow learner. You are left with a hole or void (emptiness) in your heart. Time does not heal the heart. Time will teach you to live with the emptiness. Time will teach you to adjust to the void. Knowing and communing with your Father in Heaven will remind you that you will see your loved one again.

Heavenly Father, thank you for your gift of eternal life. Thank you for sacrificing your Son so that we can have eternal life. Thank you for loving me more than life itself. Amen.

The Altar Will Alter You

Father, I Come to You

In the quiet of the night, when all the earth was still.
My Father came to me and He offered me His will.
He whispered to my heart. He beckoned to my soul.
And, this was my response to the Man Who's in
control.

Father, I come to You
with my hands lifted in praise.
Father, I come to You seeking to know
Your Will and Your Way.
Father, You promised me
You would set me free.
Father, I come to You, Father, to You.

Father, I come to You just as I am.
Father, I come to You
seeking the blood of the Lamb.
Father, please cleanse my soul.
Father, please make me whole.
Father, I come to You, Father, to You.

Oh, what a joy in coming to the Lord.
Oh, what a joy. My faith has been restored.
Oh, what a joy to know He loves me so.
Father, I come to You, Father, to You.

II Chronicles 15:2 – *"...if you seek Him, He will be found..."*

Lorraine M. Castle

Father, I Come to You – Reflections

As usual, it was late in the evening, or it could have been early morning while the moon was closing up shop and preparing to pass the baton to the sun.

I heard a whisper. "Lorraine." I ignored it. I was sleeping well without a care in the world.

"Lorraine."

"Oh, Lord," I responded. "Not now."

"Lorraine."

"Okay. Okay." I said, annoyed, as I reluctantly rose from my comfortable bed.

In the darkness, I walked into the living room. The room was brightly lit from the moonlight. The evening was quiet and peaceful. Although my flesh was agitated from being awakened, my spirit was at peace. The Spirit of the Lord could be felt all around me.

I felt like David must have felt on the hillside in the evening after his family had settled in for the night. It felt like I had the Lord all to myself. Of course, I know that the Lord is always by my side. I know that He is only a prayer away, but during the day with all the daily activities going on, when I'm surrounded by saints who also can call on His Holy Name, it's easy to feel that I'm one among many.

On this night, I knew as I had never known before that Jesus was mine! All mine! I talked to Him as a child would talk to his mother or father. I talked to Him about my

The Altar Will Alter You

aspirations and my fears – and He listened and assured me that I had nothing to fear.

As the moonlight shined through my windows and the stars twinkled in the distance, I could feel the Holy Spirit as He wrapped me in His arms, gently kissed me on my forehead, and said, "I'll be with you always."

The best part about this moment was the beginning. Jesus called my name! He called me! And, I answered. Did you answer when Jesus called your name?

Heavenly Father, thank you for calling my name! Thank you for everything you're doing in my life. Thank you for helping me to see that even though I am one among millions that I am unique in your eyes. Amen.

Lorraine M. Castle

God Will Always Be There

When you're feeling down and out
And your world fills with despair
Remember, God will bring you out.
Remember, He will always be there.

He has promised in His Word
That your burdens, He would bear.
Remember, your prayer has been heard.
Remember, God will always be there.

He was there in the Beginning.
He'll be there beyond the end.
He will lift you up, this battle He is winning.
Just hold on and don't give in.

My God provides for those who love Him.
He'll give you peace within this storm.
Just keep the Faith and place no other above Him
And watch the situation as it transforms

Remember God will bring you out.
He's the Healer of your soul.
He has all things under control.
He will be your strength when you are weak.
Within your storm, "Peace," He will speak.

Remember God will bring you out.
He holds your world within His hand.
And all your fears He will understand.
Just take it to the Lord in prayer.
He will ease your pain and all your burdens He'll bear.

The Altar Will Alter You

And when all is said and all is done
You're in the control of The Holy One.
He'll lift your burdens and despair.
Remember, God will always be there.

Hebrews 13:5 – *"I will never leave thee, nor forsake thee."*

Lorraine M. Castle

God Will Always Be There – Reflections

It turned out to be a day that I would remember for years, although I no longer remember the month. I remember that it occurred on a first Sunday. My choir sang at our communion service. It was a joyous evening of celebration. I don't remember the songs that the choir sang, but I know the songs were sung with heart-felt passion.

When I returned home, I was still basking in the glow of celebrating communion with Jesus. Unknown to me, while I basked in the glow, someone's life was in the process of being changed forever. Romans 8:28 teaches us, "that all things work together for good to them that love God, to them who are the called according to his purpose." But, as is often the case, I wasn't considering this verse when the life-altering situation that occurred in another's life was brought to my attention and neither did the individual who was the object of the change.

God is so faithful. While in my state of grieving, He gave me this poem that eased my heart. *"God Will Always Be There"* reminded me that even in times when we are feeling alone, hurt, misused, and abused, God will always be there. After God ministered to me, I was able to minister to my friend by writing and sharing this poem with my friend who was going through this transition.

God showed me by example that our gifts are not ours alone. Gifts from God are meant to be shared with His people. Are you sharing your gift with others? Allow your gift to minister to you first. When the time is right, be sure to share your gifts with God's people.

The Altar Will Alter You

Jesus, thank you for giving me words in the form of poetry to ease my pain and thank you for giving me the courage to share my gift with others. Glory to your name. Amen.

Lorraine M. Castle

God's Master Plan

God has a Master Plan
That's been in place since before time began.
God's Glory will be revealed
Through souls that He has healed.
God's Grace has set us free.
Through Him we have the victory.

God has a Master Plan.
It's time for us to stand.
We must see God's Vision through.
We have been chosen to

Feed God's children with His Word.
We must make sure each ear has heard
Of the Power and Glory of Jesus Christ.
He loved us enough to pay the ultimate price.

We are all a part of God's Master Plan
There is no time to waste.
We must share God's Plan of Salvation
With a perishing human race.

He gave His life as He hung on the tree.
We were on His mind as He died to set us free.
We must continue to tell God's Story
Until our Lord returns from Glory.

He's coming back for those
who have professed their love for Him.

He's coming back for those
who have confessed their sins to Him.

The Altar Will Alter You

He's coming back to take
those that He shepherds by the hand

To lead us to a Better Place.
It's all part of The Master's Plan.

I Peter 5:2-4 *"Feed the flock of God which is among you,
taking the oversight thereof, not by constraint, but
willingly; not for filthy lucre, but of a ready mind; Neither
as being lords over God's heritage, but being examples to
the flock. And when the chief Shepherd shall appear, ye
shall receive a crown of glory that fadeth not away."*

Lorraine M. Castle

God's Master Plan – Reflections

Sometimes we just need to be reminded that we are an intricate part of God's master plan. When faced with obstacles that weaken our inner being, it's easy to throw up our hands and give in to the obstacle. Challenges build integrity. I recall reading somewhere that we don't know how strong we are until we are challenged to the very limit. Our Plan was authored before we were conceived. When faced with a seemingly impossible task, I think on our Lord and Savior, Jesus Christ. I recall how He gave His life to save us. I remember that He knows my limitations, as well as my strengths. Additionally, I draw on scripture that tells us that He knows just how much we can bear. I think on these things, take a deep breath, praise God, and move forward with the knowledge that I am part of His Master Plan. He is with me every step of the way.

Father, I thank you for knowing me better than I know myself. I thank you for patiently guiding me on this journey we call life. I may not know every part of your plan, but I know that I am an intricate part of your plan and for this, I thank you. Amen.

The Altar Will Alter You

Highest Ground

The day has come for celebration.
Lift high the name that stands above all Creation.
Praise God and let His praises resound
As He lifts you to a higher ground.

You've passed His test with flying colors.
You've shared His love with your sisters and brothers.
You've ministered His Word so lost souls could be found
As He lifts you to a higher ground.

You've studied His Word from dusk until dawn.
While others slept, His comforting Word kept you warm.
You've accepted His challenge. In Him strength can be found
As He lifts you to a higher ground.

Stand tall brave soul. Let His Word be your light.
Be strong brave soul. Never stray from His sight.
Allow God to lead you. His foundation is sound.
He'll lead you until you've reached His Highest Ground!

Mark 16:15 – *"And he said unto them, Go ye into all the world, and preach the gospel to every creature."*

Lorraine M. Castle

Highest Ground – Reflections

God wants the best for all of His children. The path to greatness is not straight and narrow. The path is full of twists and turns, peaks and valleys, obstacles and challenges. The bible tells us that if God has given us the vision, then He has also equipped us to bring that vision to fruition. We know that's true, but at times it's difficult to remember that when we're faced with what appears to be an insurmountable obstacle. This is when we must stay prayed up and surround ourselves with like-minded people. Sometimes it's difficult to keep our eye on the prize when we are blinded with challenges. Take it to Jesus! He knows your struggles. He knows your fears and your concerns. He will provide you with everything you need to accomplish His work.

Father, thank you for trusting me with your vision. I don't deserve it. None of us do. Thank you, Jesus, for sacrificing your blood, so that I can be free to follow this vision. Thank you for holding me up and encouraging me when I wanted to stop. Thank you. Thank you. Thank you. Amen.

The Altar Will Alter You

Vision

Today I may not be
What I would like to be
But, God has given me
The ability to see
Beyond my present state
Through God's eyes I see my fate
What God has given me, is The Vision.

I see a place where we're praising the Lord
I see a place where we're spreading God's Word
I see a place where the truth can be heard
What God has given me, is The Vision.

New souls will soon be saved
In this land that God has made
He's calling us to lead
His lambs so they may feed
Continually on His Word
Until every ear has heard
What God has given me, is The Vision.

I see a place where we're praising the Lord
I see a place where we're spreading God's Word
I see a place where the truth can be heard
What God has given me
What God has given you
What God has given us, is The Vision.

Proverbs 29:18 - *"Where there is no vision the people perish."*

Lorraine M. Castle

Vision – Reflections

"Where there is no vision, the people perish (Proverbs 29:13)." Therefore, in order to survive in this world, we must have a vision. In the midst of our vision, there are distractions. There are obstacles that can hinder us and cause us to lose our focus. An analogy that can be borrowed from Corporate America is F.O.C.U.S. or Follow One Course Until Successful. Do not lose your focus. Do not take your eye off the prize. Without a vision, there is no hope. A vision does not diminish with age. It's never too late to fulfil a vision. Remember, God knows exactly how old you are. If He gives the vision to you, then He will also give you the pathway to you vision.

Father, God. Thank you for your vision. Thank you for believing in me when I couldn't or wouldn't believe in myself. Thank you for loving me enough to wait for my belief to set in. Amen.

The Altar Will Alter You

Steadfast and True

Steadfast and true
These words describe you.
You've got the love of our Lord in your heart.
For Christ you're on fire,
And through Christ you inspire
Lost souls to let God give them a new start.

You've shown by example
That God's love is ample
To fulfill every thirst and every need.
If we only abide,
In His Word we can hide
And on the bread of His life we can feed.

So, on this day of celebration.
I praise God for giving you the inspiration
To imitate the Life
Of His Son, Jesus Christ
As you spread the Gospel throughout this Nation!

Luke 16:10 – *"He that is faithful in that which is least is faithful also in much:"*

Lorraine M. Castle

Steadfast and True – Reflections

By His example, Jesus has taught us how to be steadfast and true. His desire is that we follow Him. He has given us a set of directions in His Word, the Bible. We have been commissioned to share God's Word with His children (Matthew 28:16-20). We cannot share what we what we do not have. Therefore, we must study His Word and internalize it so that we can share the love of Jesus with the world. This directive has been given to preachers and church leaders to teach us, and it's been given to the laymen (you and I). It is our duty to follow the example set forth by Jesus and share His Word throughout the land. We have been commissioned to share the story of God and all His Glory.

Heavenly Father, Thank you. Thank you for pouring into me so that I can pour into others. Thank you for your guidance and your patience. Thank you for seeing me through Christ Jesus and believing that I would follow you even when it didn't look that way to the world. Amen.

The Altar Will Alter You

If You Will Believe

If you will believe. If you will believe,
All the riches in Glory, you will receive.
If you can believe, then you will conceive
All the riches in Glory, you will receive.

You've heard it from the pastor.
And you've read it in God's Word.
You've said the name of Jesus
Is "The sweetest name you've ever heard."

You know that God delivers.
And your burdens, He'll relieve.
But my brothers and my sisters can you tell me
Do you really believe?

You know that if God gave the Vision
Then God will give the Provision.
So what's with the indecision
In moving ahead toward the Prize?

God will give you the strength to endure it.
God will give you the means to secure it.
Don't let anything try to detour it.
Keep the Faith and you will realize

That if you will believe. If you will believe,
All the riches in Glory, you will receive.
If you can believe, then you will conceive
All the riches in Glory, you will receive.

John 7:38 – *"He that believeth on me, as the scripture hath said, out of his belly shall flow rivers of living water."*

Lorraine M. Castle

If You Will Believe – Reflections

Do you believe God? I've struggled with this concept and I'm certain I'm not alone. We know the sky is blue because we can see it. We know the sun rises every day – whether the day is cloudy or not – because we have years of history to prove it. We believe what we can see, feel, touch, or smell, but how can we believe in a God that we've never seen?

We say we believe. We profess and confess to all who can hear that we believe there is a God, but deep down inside the caverns of our heart, during those lonely, midnight hours when we feel as if we are surrounded by despair – do we really believe?

We've all heard that if you believe it, you will receive it – whatever "it" may be. Does that mean that because I don't have "it," that I don't believe? We've all heard the adage that "seeing is believing." If we cannot see it, does *that* mean we don't believe?

When struggling with my unbelief, I rely on what I know. I know that we serve a living, breathing God. I know that were it not for God, I would not be here today. I draw on the miracles that God has already done in my life and in the life of others. I know that I have an inner Voice – The Holy Spirit – that gently guides me. I know that when I listen to that Voice, I'm on the right track and will never go astray.

Do I have moments when I panic because I don't feel God's presence? Of course! But, I rely on His Promise that He will never leave me or forsake me. I will never be alone. And I pray for God to help me conquer my periods of unbelief!

The Altar Will Alter You

Heavenly Father, again I ask you to help my unbelief. It is in times of despair that I need you most. When life is not treating me well, please strengthen me and keep my eye focused on you. Help me to believe and trust in you even when everything around me shouts otherwise. Help my unbelief. Amen.

My Peace

Psalm 37:11 "But the meek shall inherit the earth; and shall delight themselves in the abundance of peace."

Lorraine M. Castle

God's Love

You show His love each time you smile.
Your warmth creates a glow.
You show His love each time you speak
In a voice ever so low.

You show His love with each step you take
As you walk the Christian walk.
You show His love as you demonstrate
That walk isn't just mere talk.

You show His love in so many ways
That causes us to aspire
To follow your lead and follow God
So that He, too, will take us higher.

You show that God's love is meant to be shared
By those who seek His grace.
That we may share the glory of God
With a perishing human race.

That we may share the Gospel
With those who have lost their way
That we may all experience
The love of God you have shown today.

I John 4:11 – *"Beloved, if God so loved us, we ought also to love one another."*

The Altar Will Alter You

God's Love – Reflections

The inspiration for this poem did not set out to be an example of God's Love. In fact, operating in the background was her preference. While Jesus is the Light of the world, His light should shine through us. We never know who is watching us. Nor do we know who is looking for the love of God in us. As Christians, we have the responsibility of representing Jesus as we go through our day-to-day activities.

There will be days that are more difficult than others are and may create a challenge to allowing God's light to shine through us. Often just remembering what Jesus sacrificed for us puts it all back into perspective. What is helping another person out of a situation, or being nice to someone when my initial instinct is to withdraw, when this act is compared to Jesus giving His life for us?

We will never know what act will draw another closer to Jesus. I recall visiting a church for the first time. I didn't know anyone in the congregation. During service, we were asked to stand to pray. The elderly woman who was standing next to me grabbed my hand and squeezed it tightly in a way that I hadn't felt in the years since my grandmother passed away. That gesture brought tears to my eyes and filled my heart with love. Have you reached out and touched someone today? Never under-estimate the power of a God-filled touch.

Father, I thank you for using your children to spread your teachings and your love. Your message is so important that it is contained in every act we take. Father, please stay me focused on you because we never know who is watching us and looking for your love to shine through us. Amen.

Lorraine M. Castle

His Song

When I try to speak, there are no words
That can describe the gratitude
I feel for what He's done for me.
He's given me the victory.

When I was lost and in despair.
I thought I was beyond repair.
My God heard my unspoken plea,
And that's when Jesus rescued me.

So, I speak through His song.
The song He placed within my heart
When He gave me a brand new start.
Yes, I speak through His song,
The song I'll sing throughout eternity.

There are no words that can express
The joy I feel, the happiness
That flows throughout this soul of mine.
His love for me, His grace divine

Has lifted me. He's healed my soul.
He's placed me under His control.
How can I thank Him? There's no way.
So, I must lift my voice today.

And I speak through His song.
The song He placed within my heart
When He gave me a brand new start.
Yes, I speak through His song,
The song I'll sing throughout eternity.

Psalm 40:3 – *"...He hath put a new song in my mouth,
even praise unto our God..."*

The Altar Will Alter You

His Song – Reflections

Jesus meets us where we are. He knows our desires and He wants us to have our heart's desires (Psalm 37:4). Music has been a part of my life for as long as I can remember. While it wasn't always Christian or Gospel music, it was music none-the-less. Music always brings back fond memories. As a child, I would spend hours with my favorite uncle as he played his Jazz albums. My grandmother always had Gospel music playing on her radio. My mother enjoyed listening to rock and roll and blues music. My father listened to classical music. I loved all of it! I was drawn to church by the church choirs. I joined the church so that I could sing on the junior choir. It was the beginning of an intimate relationship that continues to this day. I've tried to describe the feeling and the intimacy I feel when singing, listening to, or even writing a song that He has given to us. Music is so therapeutic, that I'm often left with no words to adequately describe the experience. All I can do is say, "Thank You."

Jesus, thank you for music. Thank you for ushering me into your presence with music. Thank you for soothing my soul as only you can. Thank you for creating a language that we call music that is universal and transcends all generations. Thank you for Your Song. Amen.

Lorraine M. Castle

More of You, Lord

Less of me, Lord, less of me.
Less of me, Lord, less of me.
Every day, Lord, I will pray, Lord
For less of me, Lord, And more of You.

More of You, Lord, in my walk.
More of You, Lord, in my talk.
Every day, Lord, I will pray, Lord
For less of me, Lord, And more of You.

I want to start my day thinking of You,
And not of me.
Because I know only in You, Lord, will I
Have the victory.
Because I know only You, Lord, can truly
Set me free.
More of You, Lord.
More of You, Lord.
More of You, Lord.
And less of me.

Genesis 5:24 – *"Enoch walked with God: and he was not;
for God took him."*

The Altar Will Alter You

More of You, Lord – Reflections

I loved spending time with my grandmother. My grandmother would take a bus from Philadelphia, PA to New Jersey where she would pick blueberries. She would use those blueberries to make delicious pies and blueberry muffins. The first step, of course, was cleaning the blueberries, and that's where I came in. My grandmother and I would carefully separate and clean the blueberries. As we cleaned the blueberries, we ate as many as we kept for the pies and muffins. On one particular day, we ate too many blueberries and we became ill. What started out as pleasure quickly turned into temporary pain and misery. We paid the consequences of eating too many blueberries.

Isn't it wonderful that we cannot overdose on Jesus? We can never get enough of Him and I like to think that He can't get enough of us. The more of ourselves that we yield to Jesus, the more He can fill us with the power of the Holy Spirit.

Father, I thank you for taking care of our every need and desire. You are addictive and for that, I thank you. I can never get enough and you're never too much. Thank you for giving us exactly what we need. Amen.

Lorraine M. Castle

Song In My Heart

Jesus, You placed a song in my heart.
New life You gave me and a brand new start.
Your praises ring out from the depths of my soul.
My praises thank You for making me whole.
Your Spirit dwells in me and will never part.
Lord, I thank You for the song in my heart.

Jesus, You gave me joy without end.
You rescued me right when I needed a friend.
I cried out to You and You answered my call.
You lifted me and said You'll not let me fall.
You light my evenings and You're my morning star.
Lord, I thank You for the song in my heart.

You brought me through a storm.
I knew that I could count on You
To carry me through.

You kept me from all harm.
You are my everything.
You are the reason I sing.

Jesus, You placed a song in my heart.
New life You gave me and a brand new start.
Your praises ring out from the depths of my soul.
My praises thank You for making me whole.
Your Spirit dwells in me and will never part.
Lord, I thank You for the song in my heart.

Psalm 35:9 – *"And my soul shall be joyful in the Lord: it shall rejoice in his salvation."*

The Altar Will Alter You

Song in My Heart – Reflections

Jesus, You placed a song in my heart.
New life You gave me and a brand new start.
Your praises ring out from the depths of my soul.
My praises thank You for making me whole.
Your Spirit dwells in me and will never part.
Lord, I thank You for the song in my heart.

I've heard it time and time again, but I didn't believe it until it happened to me. When I turned my life over to the Lord, my troubles didn't end. I still faced challenges on a daily – sometimes minute-by-minute – basis. What changed was how I dealt with those challenges. I realized that I was no longer alone. I knew that I had an internal compass called The Holy Spirit. Tapping into that source gave me security that I didn't have when I was out in the world. That sense of security relieved my stress and anxiety and replaced it with joy.

I now understand what it means to have the joy of the Lord. I understand why that joy is my strength. When met with challenges, there are times when I am still fearful. This is when I draw on God's teachings that He has not given us the spirit of fear. I can draw on those words even though it may appear that I'm stepping into an abyss. I know that my Savior is there to protect me. He's there to catch me when I stumble. This knowledge gives me the never-ending song in my heart!

Lord, thank you for giving me your joy. Thank you for giving me the song in my heart that cannot be dampened by the storms that may exist around me. Thank you for giving me joy that does surpass all understanding. Amen.

Lorraine M. Castle

Broken

One too many words was spoken.
Now, I'm broken.

Tears of pain and tears of horror.
Feeling there is no tomorrow.
Hope is gone and I'm stricken with sorrow.
I'm broken hearted.

As I wallow in my pain
Believing I must be insane,
A light into my mind's eye came.
It's JESUS.

HE can heal my soul's diseases.
HE can mend my broken pieces.
I am freed as HE releases
HIS love for me.

HIS Spirit in me has been awakened
When I thought all had been forsaken.
I'm healed of a heart that once was breaking.
HE restoreth my soul.

HE gave HIS all to save your soul.
HE wants you under HIS control.
Your broken pieces, HE will mold
Into a brand new you.

When HE frees you – spread the WORD.
Allow HIS praises to be heard.
Continue throughout your life to serve
The ONE WHO set you free!

The Altar Will Alter You

Jeremiah 18:6 (NLB) "…As the clay is in the potter's hand, so are you in My hand…"

Lorraine M. Castle

Broken – Reflections

Have you ever felt so broken that you believed that your heart would never mend? A broken heart is devastating. It's a pain that can cut deeper than a double-edged sword. It can feel as if your heart has literally been ripped from your chest. When going through emotional stress such as a broken heart, quite often you will feel like you'll never again experience joy, and trusting another individual is inconceivable.

Jesus wants us to trust him. He will heal your broken heart. Through his word, He will teach you how to love and trust and how to be loved and trusted. Because He is the Potter and we are the clay, He will mold us as He mends our broken pieces. He will make us whole again.

Thank you, Jesus. I've thanked you a million times and that's still not enough times to thank you for loving us in our broken state. Only you can put all my broken pieces back together and for that, I will continually thank you. Amen.

The Altar Will Alter You

Time

It was time for her to go.
She knew it was time.
We knew it was time.
The time had come to travel on.

To a place where she had never been.
A place full of promise.
Promises that could not be broken.
Promises nestled in His powerful Word.

It was time for her to go.
She started down the path before.
But, she turned and ran back
To the place that held her roots.

The place that she loved.
The place where her loved ones remained.
She wanted to stay.
But she knew it was time for her to go.

I whispered in her ear
As I caressed her hand one last time.
Reminding her of the Promise.
Reminding her of the Light.

Reminding her that fear was
False Evidence Appearing Real.
Her eyelids fluttered.
She breathed a sigh of relief.

It was time for her to go.

John 8:51 – *"Verily, verily, I say unto you, If a man keep my saying, he shall never see death."*

Lorraine M. Castle

Time – Reflections

In the last years of my Mother's life, she was diagnosed with Alzheimer's and cervical cancer. When she was diagnosed with cancer, she was too frail to undergo surgery. Mom was a trooper. She did as much as she could for as long as she could. The last year of Mom's life held many sad memories, but, the joy outweighed the sorrow.

January 2009 began with my layoff from a company from which I thought I would retire. I turned 60 a few months before I was laid off. This was not a good time for me. I spent long hours looking for work to no avail. It was during this time that Mom's health began to concern us.

While I continued to look for employment, I began to realize that the time that I could spend with Mom during what we realized were her last days on this earth became more important than my search for a new job. While I continued to search for a new job, I was able to be with Mom for doctor visits, tests, diagnosis, and finally hospice home care. I was able to be to Mom what she was to me for so many years – her caregiver.

God has a way of giving us what we need when we need it. Mom was always the caregiver. She cared for us as children and adults. She cared for my Father during his illness. She cared for my great-grandmother, grandmother, and uncle during their illnesses that preceded their deaths. Because of what I initially considered an untimely lay-off, I was there with my Brother to care for Mom. It was done in God's way and in His time.

The Altar Will Alter You

Heavenly Father, I thank you for allowing me to give my Mother just what she needed in her final days on this earth. Thank you for making a way out of no way. Thank you for keeping your promise to never leave us or forsake us. Amen.

Lorraine M. Castle

Brand New

Today is the beginning of a brand new day.
I'm praising my Savior in a brand new way.
I'm praising my Savior in a brand new place.
I'm praising my Savior face to face.

So, don't be sorrowful. No, don't shed a tear.
I am at rest now with my Jesus so near.
I can reach out and touch Him as I worship Him here.
I'm so glad I pressed on; so glad I persevered.

I know you will miss me and I will miss you.
But earth is just a rest stop that we must pass through
On the way to our prepared destination
Where my soul can run free in its full restoration.

If you love my Jesus, then I will see you again
And we'll praise the Lord together as we join Him in His
reign
Over all of Heaven and all of the Earth
As we celebrate earthly death and our Heavenly birth.

Today is the beginning of a brand new day.
I'm praising my Savior in a brand new way.
I'm praising my Savior in a brand new place.
I'm praising my Savior face to face.

3rd John 1:14 – *"But I trust I shall shortly see thee, and we shall speak face to face."*

The Altar Will Alter You

Today she would be referred to as My Bestie or BFF. Her Aunt had recently passed away and she was responsible for preparing the funeral program. Of course, she knew I wrote poetry. She asked me if I could write a poem to place on the funeral program. You would have thought this would have been a simple request because I write poetry. But, I couldn't find the right words.

I labored before the Lord asking Him to give me the right words. Days passed and I still didn't have a poem. Would I have to tell my best friend that she would have to find a poem on her own – at the last minute? As always, God was right on time. At what I perceived to be the 11th hour, words began to pour from my thoughts, to my heart, to my fingers, to paper. While **Brand New** was written for my friend, it was written for anyone who has ever had a loved one who transitioned. "To be absent from the body is to be present with the Lord." (II Corinthians 5:8)

Heavenly Father, I thank you for fulfilling my need. You know just what I need and you know when I need it.

Author's Bio

Lorraine McCray Castle

Lorraine Castle was born and raised in Philadelphia, PA. She was educated in the Philadelphia Public School System. She went on to attend LaSalle University in Philadelphia, PA and Cabrini College in Radnor, PA where she majored in Accounting, Finance and Organizational Management. Most recently, Lorraine attended the University of Phoenix where she acquired her undergraduate degree in Communications with an emphasis on Technology.

With a heart and love for writing, Lorraine was President of the P.E.N. Warriors (Purposed to Edify the Nation) and L-Y-N-X (Lyrics You'd Never Expect), two writing teams at Bethany Baptist Church in Lindenwold, New Jersey where she has participated in writing plays, poetry, devotionals, testimonies and short stories. After retiring, in 2010 Lorraine began a virtual assistance company that assists authors with editing, manuscript preparation, and formatting books for print and eBooks.

Today Lorraine resides in Lindenwold, New Jersey where she attends Bethany Baptist Church under the teachings of Bishop David G. Evans. Feel free to visit Lorraine's website at www.castlevirtualsolutions.com.

Follow Lorraine on Facebook, Twitter, or LinkedIn

https://www.facebook.com/Lorraine-M-Castle-Author-433347353536006/?ref=hl

https://twitter.com/ABCWordsmith

Lorraine M. Castle

http://www.linkedin.com/in/lorrainecastle/

Email Lorraine: lorraine@castlevirtualsolutions.com

Sign up for Lorraine's newsletter *Write On* to receive a gift of two poems from an upcoming book at http://www.castlevirtualsolutions.com/

Other Books by Lorraine McCray Castle

"*Turn Writing Your Book Into a Marketing Success*" – Lorraine's free eBook can be downloaded at www.castlevirtualsolutions.com.

Books that Lorraine contributed to:

"*It's a God Thing: Stories to Help You Experience the Heart of God*" Available on Amazon.com

"*Seek Your Peak to Find Your Spark*" Available on Amazon.com

Coming Soon – "*On the Edge of a Miracle*" – A collection of Christian poetry

Coming Soon – "*The JOY of Christmas*" – A collection of poetry for the Christmas season

Coming Soon – "*Blessings Found in a 6 Letter Word*" – An anthology by Breast Cancer Survivors and their Caregivers

www.ingramcontent.com/pod-product-compliance
Lightning Source LLC
LaVergne TN
LVHW011333080426
835513LV00006B/329